Saved By His Amazing Grace

He Never Gave Up On Me

Monna Ellithorpe

ISBN-13:
978-1986446884

ISBN-10:
1986446883

Table of Contents

God's Children

Ever since I was a child living and growing up in a small town in Ohio, I can remember my Mom taking me to church and continued even after we moved to Florida.

I remember my grandfather and grandmother (step-grandmother as my real grandmother had already passed away) were always at church.

I was raised in the Pentecostal faith and some of my remembrances were and are still very scary when I think back on them.

If you are not familiar with the Pentecostal church, there are some differences between their practices and other religions such as Catholic, Methodist, Lutheran, Protestant, etc. Back then, I didn't know there was any other different way of worshipping God.

I actually used to stand up in front of the church congregation and sing gospel songs with my Mom. In fact, I still have my Mom's collection of the old time gospel songs in her handwriting.

I don't have that kind of confidence to sing in front of people now. Maybe if I had continued to practice singing, I would feel differently now but I can't sing worth anything these days.

Maybe I couldn't then either but the Bible says in Psalm 98:4 King James Version (KJV), "Make a joyful noise unto the Lord." I must have been doing that; good or not.

The one thing I remember was the "speaking in tongues" (1 Corinthians 14:2), which scared the bejeebers out of me. I don't remember Mom explaining that to me ahead of time and it was very scary.

I didn't know if the people were losing their minds, on drugs or possessed by the devil or what was going on.

Mom explained it to me later after the service. In the Pentecostal religion when someone speaks in tongues, this is the Lord speaking through them. Even though I never watched the movie The Exorcist all the way through this reminded me of that and I knew there was no way I wanted to be controlled like that.

My grandfather was a big leader in the church and was a part of almost everything that happened from the services to the singing to arranging the "tent meetings."

My cousin Kay and I went to those almost every night and we were just so bored and scared of everything.

I remember Mom watching the Reverend Billy Graham on TV. Sadly he just passed away recently (2/21/2018) at the age of 99.

Roman Catholic Bishop Fulton Sheen was referred to as the "first televangelist" but I always thought it was Billy Graham.

My Dad didn't go to church and he didn't object when Mom took me to church with her. He called them "Holy Rollers" and I never really understood what he meant by that either but I believe it was meant as a derogatory remark. "Sorry, Dad if I'm wrong."

Fast forward: My Dad did have the presence of mind to ask God for His forgiveness before he passed on.

The older I got, the more I resisted going to church with my Mom until I discovered boys. I didn't mind it so much then when I could see the boys I liked.

When you're in your early teens or as it was for me, I didn't think much of life, death, being a Christian or any part of what might happen if the world came to an end.

I knew I didn't like to hear about it and to tell you the truth; I still don't like to hear about the end of the world as we know it, even at the age of 60.

Although I have not lived my life as a born again Christian, what I learned and what I was taught in Sunday School and Vacation Bible School has always stayed with me in the back of my heart and my mind. I've tried to live my life the best that I can and be a good person.

I'm not sure if I'm considered the normal or not but as I progressed into my later teens; 16, 17, 18, I did experiment with alcohol, drugs and sex. I put the lessons that I had been taught in the back of my mind and lived my life the way I wanted to.

I knew it wasn't what my mother or my family of Christians would want for me but at that age, I guess many of us think we are untouchable, invincible and indestructible and that nothing could happen to us.

I became like my Dad in many ways. He was a good man but he just didn't want to hear about religion or anything like that.

Maybe it scared him to an extent too and that's how he dealt with it and it's also how I dealt with it.

I didn't like to hear about the terrible things that were going to happen if you weren't a Christian.

I look back on it now and see that the Pentecostal faith was very aggressive and most of the members were determined that they were going to convince you and everyone else that you would "burn in Hell" if you did not follow God's word.

This was too much for me to comprehend and so I stopped going to church when I was old enough to make my own decisions.

I knew I could not commit to being perfect, so I didn't try.

It wasn't until years later that I finally realized that serving God isn't an either or proposition.

I didn't understand that God knows humans will make mistakes and if they continued to learn and repent of their sins and try to live a Christian life; all is well.

I still prayed when I needed things and hoped that God would give them to me or see things my way but I had no right to do that but again my understanding was clouded.

Call it intervention by the devil or stubbornness on my part that made me the way I was. I did try to be a good person; if you overlooked the alcohol, drugs and sex.

I did have my own boundaries that I did not cross and didn't like to be around people who crossed the rules I had set for myself.

Not that I tried to force anyone to see things my way, these were my rules I followed.

As an example, I would "NEVER" use the name of the Lord in vain or speak of God in a bad way but I just wouldn't follow Him like my family did.

I think back now and see so many times things happened to me that were not the way I wanted it to be and I couldn't figure out, "Why would God ignore me? I'm a good person."

I decided it was just another reason for me to turn away from God because like a spoiled child, I didn't get my way or what I wanted.

I kept on living my life the way I wanted to live and for the most part I did have a good life. I was never beaten or abused in any way.

Mom and Dad made sure I had everything I needed without spoiling me too much, so I thought "Why do I need God?" I never said those words out loud to anyone but that's what my thoughts amounted to.

But believe me when things weren't going good, who did I call on to help me out? Yep, it was God.

How could I be so selfish and cry out for help when I was not living my life as a Christian?

I talked my way through each and every occurrence or so I made myself believe I had gotten away with something and I kept on living life as I wanted to.

I thought I was smart. I knew all about how I should be living my life but in the meantime I was going to have fun and when it came my time to pass from this earth, I'd have enough time to ask forgiveness for all of my sins and God would just take me in without a second thought.

I'm thinking now that there are probably many people who think the same way and maybe there are times that a person will have the time to ask God for His forgiveness and they would be allowed to enter the Gates of Heaven.

Will You Have Enough Time?

My husband Rea (pronounced Ray) was raised pretty much in the same way that I was and he lived his life so much like I had been doing.

He remembered his religious roots and what he had been taught and believed that he would have the time to ask God to forgive him when his time came.

I actually do believe that is what happened that early Sunday morning in August of 2008 when my husband asked God for His forgiveness and then my precious husband took his last breath. I know the earthly love of my life is with God in Heaven right now.

My husband served 30 years in the Army as a proud Airborne Ranger and was in so much pain from his injuries and the guilt feelings.

Many times I know he wanted to end it all so he could be out of pain and not have those horrible memories haunt him each day and night but he was raised that suicide is a sin and he would never do that.

He was haunted all of the time, living and remembering the things he saw and the things he was ordered to do.

He told me once he did not think God would ever forgive him for any of the sins he had committed.

It has to be a heavy burden for any of our military soldiers to do what is against their beliefs but they also want to serve and protect our country and the people.

I think there is a fine line between following orders in war, versus doing something wrong that you decide to do because of evilness.

My husband was not evil and he did as he was ordered to do. I know my husband did ask forgiveness for any sins he committed during war time and I believe God does forgive if one is truly repenting of the sin, no matter how it came about or happened.

I'm somewhat off topic a bit but this just came to mind and I wanted to make sure I added this line of thought.

Regrets

As I think back on things in my life, I see and have so many regrets. "What would my life be like now if I had made better or different choices?"

My first husband went through a time where he also tried to follow God as a Christian. I still resisted at that time. How different would things have been?

Would we have stayed married or would things have turned out the same as they have already?

I have turned my life over to God many times but each time it turned out to be promises that I didn't keep and I was so ashamed.

I had every intention of following the Lord as a Christian but I let the devil draw me back into his world.

I know God has forgiven me for the wrong that I

have done and I am "Blessed" by being forgiven. I would never have dreamed that I would be writing a book about my thoughts and my life in and out of Christianity.

There are still so many unanswered questions I have and I'm not sure how to get the answers.

I'm told to read the Bible but with all due respect, I get lost in what is being said when I try to read the Bible.

I have bought a few different Bibles that are easier to understand but I wonder, "Am I reading God's word in a more simple and understandable language that I can understand or am I reading someone else's interpretation of the Bible?"

There are so many different translations of the Bible now:
NIV: New International Version
NAB: New American Bible
HCSB: Holman Christian Standard Bible

NASB: New American Standard Bible

KJV: King James Version

NKJV: New King James Version

NRSV: New Revised Standard Version

ESV: English Standard Version

NIrV: New International Reader's Version

NLT: New Living Translation

CEV: Contemporary English Version

NCV: New Century Version

The Message: A Paraphrase

AMP: Amplified Bible

All of these versions and their definitions I received in a pamphlet from my local Christian book store. The pamphlet is from Zondervan Bibles.

Who is to say that each religion or translation is correct in their beliefs and interpretations or does God recognize and accept the different practices of the different religions?

For example:

Catholic – according to Webster's New Basic Dictionary and Thesaurus, it's defined as Catholic is universal; including the whole body of Christians; relating to the Roman Catholic Church.

There are practices that the Catholics follow that I've never been taught and I don't understand.

As far as I know, the Pentecostal religion is the only one who recognizes "speaking in tongues."

There are some people (atheists) who do not believe there is a God at all.

This book is not about whether there is a God or not.

This book is about my beliefs that there *__"IS"__* a God and my choice to live a Christian life and how I've come to see things differently in my trials along the way.

If you don't believe there is a God, that is your choice

and you can write your book some day.

I may feel differently as time goes on but I'm still not an outspoken person when it comes to debating anything religious or political that I believe in.

I don't have the confidence yet to do that.

If I feel that I can say or share something of my Christian belief with someone that I think may help them, I will share it with them but I will not continue to push my beliefs on anyone.

Now maybe some will say that if I truly believe in God and want to live my life in a Christian way, then I would have no problem with telling people about God.

Hmmm, I'm doing that here but I'm not going to try and make anyone buy this book.

I will advertise this book and put it out there for people to read but I still do not believe that "harping or nagging" over and over about anything to anyone is going to make any difference.

For me in the past and even now, someone with a very aggressive agenda to make someone "see the light" drives me further away from what people are trying to talk to me about.

Still a bit of the "bratty child" in me, I guess.

Of course now that I have made the choice and asked Jesus to become my Lord and Saviour, I want to learn all I can and do the best that I can to follow His word.

Angry With God

Many times I have been upset with God about the way things have happened but I can honestly say that I was never truly angry or mad at God until the morning I lost my husband of two days.

Even now, almost ten years later, I still don't understand, nor do I fully accept that there was a good reason he was taken away from me so soon.

Often, I've felt just because I wasn't living right, I was being punished.

I lost my husband, our home we lived in together, my car and my job and still I was angry. I had finally let someone take care of me. Now he was gone and all of those plans we had made to grow old together was not going to happen as we thought they would or at all.

If I had kept going to church, I would still have my husband. If I had done this or that or other things differently or right, he wouldn't have been taken away from me.

I don't know how to explain it any better, other than I hated God for taking my husband away and I wanted nothing to do with Him at all.

If he were truly a loving God my husband would still be here with me.

I still struggle with being upset at times but I don't hate God or think that I was singled out for any reason other than He was trying to get my attention and it was time to finally trust in Him and follow Him and His word.

I've learned that God doesn't punish anyone that way and not until now did I understand that I looked to the wrong person to take care of me.

God guides our lives if and when we let Him and the earthly man is the protector.

I am learning to thank God for letting me meet my

Rea, fall in love again and cherish the times that we did have together.

I was able to experience what love and commitment to another person is supposed to be like. The previous 30 years before that, I had only been subjected to what a bad marriage can be like.

My first husband was not a bad person. We were both too young and too immature to be in a marriage. I do thank God and my former husband for the beautiful daughter that we were given from our union.

This is another lesson that life and age has taught me. We make our own choices whether good or bad and they may turn out to be good choices or bad choices but they were our choices that we made and no one is to blame but ourselves.

I don't blame my ex-husband for everything that went wrong in our marriage; I blame "US" for things not working out.

As I mentioned earlier in this book, I set rules for myself and I worried that getting a divorce was a sin and that I would not be forgiven for that but I also thought that God would not want two people to continue to live together and try to raise a child when we were fighting and arguing all of the time.

We did divorce and I think my daughter became a better person by not being exposed, raised or living in such an unhappy environment.

Pre-Destined Events or Things Just Happen

Some people believe that everything in life happens as a pre-destined event and some people think things just happen and one thing causes another event to happen.

Looking back on my own life, I can see where things have happened that could be supported by both theories but I tend to lean more to the pre-destined events are set in motion the moment we are born.

There are so many things that happen in your life; some are life altering events and some are so small that they are not worth mentioning at the time but later you will see even the small events has had some kind of an impact on you and your future.

Fearless Teenage Years

I sometimes wonder how I made it through my teen years and even some years after that without becoming an alcoholic, a drug addict, maimed or even killed.

Driving drunk, driving under the influence of drugs; sometimes alcohol and drugs together and I still made it out alive and without killing anyone else.

God had a plan for my life, even though I didn't know it or even care at the time. So many bad choices that I made should have resulted in my death years ago but I'm still here to write this book.

I don't claim to know all the answers, I'm just writing a book explaining things in my life that led me to where I am today.

I hope that my words will resonate with someone who may have led somewhat of a parallel life to mine and that they may turn to God for guidance as I do now, each and every day.

So Many Prayers, Hopes and Wishes

How many times have you "prayed?"

"God, please let me get this job?"

"God, please let me have that promotion."

"God, please get me through this hangover and I'll never drink again."

I've been there myself, lots of times. Sometimes I got the job, sometimes I didn't and of course I did live through the hangovers and eventually never drank again.

But not once do I remember thanking God for answering even one of those prayers that I so nonchalantly prayed for.

Be honest, you've done the same thing, haven't you?

I'm not passing judgment, just making an educated

guess.

It seems that the reverence that God is due has fallen by the wayside and has for many years.

Love of God and Country are no longer a priority to people and sadly it's not taught to the children like it used to be when I started out in school.

True, being an American does give us the freedom of speech but so many liberties have been reduced to no more than a passing thought. There is no longer any respect or reverence given to God or Country like it was years ago.

Even though I haven't led my life as Christian-like as I should have, I still knew right from wrong.

Why aren't we teaching our children about God and about patriotism and the basic laws of our land and yes, even the world?

Some countries do have different laws, values and a

sense of God and Country that are far different than the normal things we were taught but I still have faith that most people, down deep have a sense of right and wrong and practice some sort of faith.

Living in Faith and Trusting God

I've struggled with faith so much in my life. I've always heard that "God helps those who help themselves."

But if we are supposed to have faith that God will handle things for us, then how do we know when to just let God take control or should we be doing something to help ourselves?

One day, not too long ago I had a situation in my life that I had no idea what to do about it.

How was I supposed to know the ideas that came to me were the guidance that God was giving me or was it something I was trying to manipulate to have the outcome be what I wanted it to be?

Just like raising children, there isn't a "Life Manuel" or is there? The Bible is supposed to have every answer to any question that we could ever ask but when you cannot understand the language or you get lost in the meaning of the words, where do you turn?

I know, the Bible also tells us that, "God will not give us more than we can handle."

But when you don't know how to handle it or what to do, what happens then?

It took me a long time to be able to just let go, have faith in God and let Him handle things. I had always been used to taking care of things myself.

I had or what I thought was total control of every situation concerning my life and giving up that "so called control" was hard but for the first time in my life, I had to start having faith; total and complete faith that God would look out for me.

I also wondered if I was just playing a silly game. I'll tell God this and I'll get what I want and then I'll still live my life the way I want to.

It just doesn't work that way and I knew that.

Out of Time, Chance Number One

No matter how prepared you think you are or will be, you just never know if you will have the time or the presence of mind at the time to ask God for forgiveness.

September 3, 2017, a normal day with the exception that my daughter had remarried a few days earlier and was on her honeymoon cruise while I stayed at her house to look after my grandbabies (still my babies at 16 and 12 at the time I write this book).

Sunday morning I woke up, watched Joel Osteen on the TV as I have done every Sunday morning now for the last few years. My grand-daughter and grand-son were with their Dad and would be coming to the house later in the day.

I decided to take a shower and relax the rest of the day until they came home so we could be together as we went through the hurricane they named Irma and it was making its way toward us.

The hurricane was taking its sweet time in reaching Florida, so I worried about my daughter and her new husband on their honeymoon cruise; "Would they be able to get home safely before the hurricane made landfall?"

As I mentioned, pretty much a normal Sunday until I made one wrong step in the shower and down I went. I attempted to grab onto something to break my fall but there was nothing to hold on to except the shower curtain.

I hit hard on my right side, hip, back; right arm and finally my head hit the edge of the shower opening and I pulled the shower curtain down on top of me.

I remember thinking how much it hurt when my head hit the edge of the shower wall. The shower curtain rod hurts when you get hit in the head with that too.

I knew I had not lost consciousness but I wasn't quite sure why. I felt the "goose egg" starting to get bigger on the right side of my head just behind my ear and the pain everywhere else.

I stayed there on the shower floor for a few minutes trying to figure out how I was going to get up. My ankle, leg and hip hurt and I sure didn't want to slip and fall again.

I found that I could reach the towel that I was going to use and thought if I could put it on the shower floor I could get up without slipping again.

I got up very slow and very carefully. I washed the shampoo out of my hair and the soap off of my body as best as I could. I needed to get out of that shower and sit down.

I just kept thinking that I was so thankful that I wasn't bleeding from my head or anywhere else and that my grand-babies wouldn't be coming home to find me unconscious or dead.

I probably should have gone to the Emergency Room to be checked out but I didn't. I was almost positive that I had a concussion. My head hurt like no other headache I'd ever had before but I stayed awake and made it through the rest of the day.

I wasn't going to tell my grand-babies what had happened but decided they should know just in case something happened after I went to sleep.

Thinking back, I realized I could've been **"Out Of Time."**

I did not have a chance to ask God for forgiveness of my sins. I very well could have died that morning and as good of a person that I had tried to be, I wondered if it had been enough.

I thanked God for not letting me die or be hurt more than I was that morning and life went on.

Out Of Time, Chance Number Two

It was time to start preparing for Hurricane Irma to hit us but she kept moving towards the east and then towards the west and growing bigger and bigger.

Hurricane Irma hit our Fort Myers, Florida shores on Sunday, September 10, 2017 in the early afternoon.

She had grown to be a massive hurricane, estimating it to be at least 400 miles wide which almost totally covered the entire State of Florida.

Fort Myers did not take a direct hit but we were hit from the back and right side which is said to be the worst and most dangerous part of a hurricane.

My grand-babies and I were safely hid away in an inside closet at my home. I had such a strong feeling that would be the safest place for us to be.

We would've been evacuated from my daughter's house if we had tried to stay there.

We watched the news on TV and got our updates on the hurricane from our cell phones until about 2:43 pm EST, when we lost power and only had sporadic cell phone service.

We had brought in blankets, pillows, snacks and games with us in the closet and considering there was a hurricane outside, we actually had a pretty good time together, talking, laughing and being silly.

I had turned everything over to God and I knew there was nothing I could do but what I had already done to keep my grand-babies safe.

I prayed that my daughter and her new husband would be safe on the cruise ship that had gone back to Cozumel, Mexico to stay out of the path of the hurricane.

My grand-kids and I watched the hurricane for most of the afternoon through the open door of the closet and out the window.

A few hours into our hide-away in the closet, the winds and rains were getting worse so I had my grandson close the closet door and we waited and listened. We could hear the wind and rain but we weren't scared. I wanted to keep as calm as I could so my grand-kids would not be upset or scared.

The sounds outside seemed to be subsiding so my grandson slowly opened the closet door so we could look out and see what was going on. It was very calm, very still and almost as if there was nothing there.

I told my grandson to quickly shut the door and get back inside because the eye of the hurricane was passing over us and the backside of a hurricane is more dangerous and fierce with stronger winds and rain.

We spent I believe a total of about eight to ten hours in that closet together. I knew in my heart we were safe and that my daughter and her new husband were safe too.

I made it a point to "Thank God" for seeing us safely through the hurricane and explaining to my grandchildren that I had prayed and asked God to look out for all of us and He did.

It was as if God had put his hands over the house that day and protected all of us. We saw and heard strong winds and rain but we were safe.

There was absolutely no damage to the house and we lost maybe two plants in front of the house. Again, I thanked God for keeping us safe.

We survived Hurricane Irma by God's grace and "me" here on earth to do what I needed to do to get us through the storm and to comfort the kids and keep myself calm.

Correction: That is how I felt before I gave it all to God to handle. I was still new to letting God handle everything and I felt like I was the only one that could get us through, here on earth.

Those hours closed up in the closet, I had the most amazing feeling of calmness and the feeling of God's hands surrounding this house and that we were safe.

My only daughter and my new son in law were still on their honeymoon out in the ocean where the hurricane had started and they could not get home to be with us.

Again, I turned that worry and stress over to God and I "just knew" they were safe and they would be home safe as soon as they could get here.

Out Of Time, Chance Number Three

The next morning we woke up still somewhat exhausted and bleary-eyed from the events of the day and night before.

We survived the hurricane, only to be involved in a five car crash while on our way to check on my daughter's house.

I found myself standing in the middle of the road with five crashed vehicles, my grandson okay, my grand-daughter having a major anxiety attack and hyperventilating and not knowing yet if she was injured or not. She was a new driver of only about 5 or 6 months.

I didn't know if I was injured because I was so concerned about my grand-babies and I looked up to Heaven and asked God, "What am I suppose to learn from this?"

I did, however, remember to thank God that we were

not killed or hurt any more than we were.

How do you make sense of the events of the last eleven days? I found myself relying more and more on the fact that I could not handle this on my own and that even this event would have to be left in God's hands.

As confusing as it was, there had to be a reason for this; still not sure what it was but I was keeping faith that the reason would eventually be shown to me.

I had been worried about my grand-daughter's driving and thought maybe this was a way to make her more aware of how dangerous driving a car can be if you text by phone, talk on the phone or just don't pay close attention to your driving.

Did I make a wrong decision about driving to my daughter's house to see if there was damage so soon? Should we have waited longer to go check on the house?

For the second time in a week I could have been or any one of us could have been seriously hurt or killed in the accident or my daughter and new son in law could have been hit by Hurricane Irma while on that cruise ship.

You know what? Again, I didn't have time to ask God to forgive me of my sins and ask that He become my Lord and Saviour like I always thought I would have time to do for the majority of my life.

Things happen way too fast to count on being able to ask for forgiveness in a split second between possible life and death.

Las Vegas Mass Shooting

Of the 50+ people who were killed and over 500 injured in Las Vegas on October 1, 2017, how many do you think had the time to repent of their sins and ask for God's forgiveness before they were gunned down?

The majority of those people I would almost certainly say had no idea whatsoever that they only had minutes left to live.

This world is getting scarier each and every day to live in. Think of the list of violence and natural disasters all across the world, from events of weather, fires, suicide bombers, the shooting of individuals to killing great numbers of people at a time.

This Nation (The United States of America) was founded under God. Why are we allowing the devil to impose his evil power over us and not holding God, life, liberty and justice to our hearts as was intended?

The original Pledge of Allegiance was written in August of 1892 by socialist minister Francis Bellamy and at that time, the pledge did not mention God.

It wasn't until 1954 that President Dwight D. Eisenhower encouraged Congress to add "In God we Trust" to the pledge as we know it today and now some want it removed and I think that's just wrong but that is another topic for another book.

The Pledge of Allegiance

"I pledge allegiance to the Flag of the United States of America, and to the Republic for which it stands, one Nation under God, indivisible, with liberty and justice for all."

I was raised to respect God, the flag, our Nation, our President and all the freedom that we had because of the sacrifices that many American soldiers had fought and died for and still do to this day.

I'm getting off topic again but you see, God has been a huge part of my life since I was very young, even though I tried to deny Him many times. He never gave up on me.

My Later Years

I have always tried to be a good person all of my life but I also had the feeling I was never getting anywhere and I would be homeless and destitute in my declining years.

I lived paycheck to paycheck most of the time and I didn't seem to see any way to change that.

In looking back through events in my life, both good and bad, I see there were many times that I had the money for what I needed but I never could quite figure out how it came to be or why.

I see now, it was God watching over me. Even though I'd turned my back on Him, He never gave up on me.

I had worked for a very well known and lucrative company for many years when I was younger but as the downsizing came about in the 1980s, I was let go from the job I thought I would retire from.

From then on I went from job to job, again being let go due to downsizing.

My best friend and I took classes at the local Vocational School and learned medical transcription.

We had researched and realized that there is always a need for doctors, hospitals and medications, so surely this would be a thriving occupation for many years to come and it was for a while.

Years down the road, the medical professionals decided they could use automation at less cost than paying us to type their reports for them.

I was out of a good paying job again, about a month after my husband passed away.

So without going through every detailed part of my life, the point I'm trying to make is that I had some rough times and even though I wasn't living as I should, it seemed that God saw in me something worth believing in and he kept helping me all along.

How else would anyone explain the positive things that happened in my life, even amidst the negative events?

For the last six years I have been caregiver to my second mom who has Alzheimer's Disease and I've been fortunate enough to have a beautiful home to live in while caring for her.

I give thanks to God and to her for the place to live and the opportunity to finally go after my dream of writing.

So now I've reached the age of 60, a widow with no permanent home to live in, no car to drive but I am writing and I will soon be launching my course and ideas online.

I know there has to be many people out there just like me with the same questions and doubts.

I believe God had this planned all along. I had no idea or indication that my life would have taken the path that it has. "No." It wasn't my call to make.

Don't misunderstand, I made good and bad choices but the bad choices were because I didn't trust God enough to take care of my life for me.

I thought I had to be the one to do it all.

This reminds me of a poem that I've heard all of my life. It's sad that we really don't know who the original author is but the version I know was written by Carolyn Carty in 1963 and called "Footprints" but I've also known it to be titled

---

"Footprints in the Sand"

One night a man had a dream. He dreamed he was walking along the beach with the LORD. Across the sky flashed scenes from his life. For each scene he noticed two sets of footprints in the sand. One belonging to him and the other to the LORD.

When the last scene of his life flashed before him, he

looked back at the footprints in the sand. He noticed that many times along the path of his life there was only one set of footprints. He also noticed that it happened at the very lowest and saddest times of his life.

This really bothered him and he questioned the LORD about it.

LORD you said that once I decided to follow you, you'd walk with me all the way.

But I have noticed that during the most troublesome times in my life there is only one set of footprints.

I don't understand why when I needed you most you would leave me.

The LORD replied, "*My precious, precious child, I Love you and I would never leave you! During your times of trial and suffering when you see only one set of footprints, it was then that I carried you.*"

I can now see that has been the pathway of my life.

Even when I didn't realize it, God was carrying me at my lowest times.

Will You Have Faith and Let God Take Control?

I still have many, many questions that I know I may never find the answers to but with the help of God, I will live my life according to His word and work every day to be thankful for what I have and the strength to have faith to let Him handle things.

I'm not perfect. I don't propose to be and I know I will make mistakes but I know and understand now; just because you are a Christian and a child of God, you won't be perfect.

You will make mistakes and you will have some doubts and you will be forgiven.

Just remember that God is a loving and forgiving God and as long as you are sincere and really trying to live your life by His Word and the Bible, then things will be okay.

Ask Him for guidance, I do every day now and many times a day.

Do I still wonder if I'm keeping an open mind enough to hear His voice or is it my voice I'm trying to convince myself is right?

Is it the devil trying to pull me back into the mean and evil part of his world?

James 4:7

"Submit yourselves therefore to God. Resist the devil, and he will flee from you."

Psalm 37:4 New International Version (NIV)

"Take delight in the LORD, and he will give you the desires of your heart."

You'll Know When God Speaks To You (Update)

I wrote this book back in October of 2017 and it is now March of 2018 and Yes, I am a born again Christian, a child of God and letting God lead my way and my faith in Him grows stronger every day.

Earlier in this book, I mentioned about not knowing if God was speaking to me or if I was trying to convince myself of something.

For the last few months, I've faithfully read the Bible every night and prayed daily about many things.

I didn't know if I was doing what God wanted me to do or not.

So many times being a new Christian, I wondered if I had missed the message I was to receive from God.

What if I had convinced myself that I was living God's plan for my life and it was the devil luring me back to my old ways?

And then one day things changed and there was no doubt whatsoever that I felt the presence of God or heard the voice of God in my heart, but it was all clear to me what I was to do and it came in His time.

I wrote this next section about five days ago... (February 23, 2018).

Since I've gotten saved again, I've been struggling with trying to understand what God tells me versus what I'm telling myself.

I just keep praying every day that He will show me what I am to do.

The other morning, I got up and out of bed and it just came to me.

There was a sense of reassurance that came over me and there was my answer.

My friend Brenda, stated, "You got a revelation" after I explained to her what happened.

It was a clear message that came to me;

"I've provided the finances and cleared the way for you, now go and write your stories."

I stood there for a minute and I asked, God

"Is it that simple?"

And I felt, heard or sensed (not sure how to explain it) but it was a definite, *"Yes, it's that simple."*

So I'm now concentrating on writing for my blog and my books.

I told Brenda, "It was an amazing feeling and I also saw her on that journey with me.

So I think He's having us look out for each other."

Brenda has been instrumental in helping me learn and keep the faith and I thank her so much for that.

Billy Graham, "America's Pastor"

As mentioned earlier in this book, Billy Graham passed away on February 21, 2018.

I watched his funeral online and something that he said in one of the film clips of his crusades really made me think.

I'm always wondering if and when I'll understand what I'm reading in the Bible.

Billy Graham stated:

"It's a strange thing about this book (the Bible). There are many things in it I don't understand and can't explain. Some of the questions I have asked about it I am sure will never be answered this side of Heaven."

If a man like Billy Graham had questions about the Bible, then I'm surely not going to find all of the answers.

All I can do is the best I can to love God, follow His teachings and keep the faith and let Him handle the things in my life.

I can't do it on my own and it sure gives you a feeling

of peacefulness and calmness to know that you are never alone as long as you ask Jesus to come into your life.

It's funny how things come about when you are focused on something.

Now that I have been born again, I see so many inspiring and helpful videos, articles and posts, etc. about Jesus, God and faith.

Where Was God?

There was another tragic school shooting at Marjory Stoneman Douglas High School in Parkland, Florida on February 14, 2018; Valentine's Day of all days.

There were 17 students and teachers killed and many others wounded. Since that day two more victims have died.

People wonder and ask, "God, where were you when this happened to all of these people?"

If you will remember, God and religion has been taken out of our schools as it offends some people.

On June 17, 1963 – the Supreme Court declared school-sponsored prayer and Bible readings unconstitutional.

I'll tell you, He was still with the victims even though He's been banned from schools. He was there with each victim, holding them and comforting them.

We all make our own choices but then we want to blame God and others when things turn out wrong or tragic.

God was even with the shooter that day. The shooter

had the choice to do this evil deed or walk away.

He followed through with his plans. He did not walk away when God gave him the chance.

Satan and pure evil led this young man to take that automatic weapon and turn it on the people of the school.

Billy Graham's passing, just a week after the shooting; do you think that just happened?

"No!"

Billy Graham has said for a long time he was ready to meet his Creator.

Do you think its a coincidence that one of, if not **THE** most famous preachers of the gospel of all time is again brought before us as a faithful servant of God.

Even in death, Reverend Graham helped to spread the word of God to the world through his children as they remembered their father.

We had to have a crusader of God's word to remind us how desperately we need to bring God and prayer back to our schools, to our children and everyone from all walks of life.

Kathie Lee Gifford, long time co-anchor of the Today Show has always made it well-known that she is a born again Christian and believes in the word of God, along with our Vice President, Mike Pence.

Satan is working over-time when other celebrities chose to make fun of the Vice President and all others who believe in God.

I will pray for our leaders, our Nation, our Country, all of the people of this great land and "Yes," I'll also pray for those who are non-believers.

The violence, hate and pettiness needs to "STOP" and it needs to stop NOW!

This is my story of how I came back to Jesus Christ and turned my life completely over to him.

I pray that something I've said will bring even one person to re-think how they are living their life.

Trust and have faith in Jesus Christ. For our children's sake as well as every person on earth.

We need to freely ask Jesus Christ to help us.

I was ***"Saved By His Amazing Grace"*** three times in September of 2017.

How about you?

Satan cannot dwell in a mind or body that has asked Christ to walk with them.

The following scripture is worth repeating.

James 4:7

Submit yourselves, then, to God. Resist the devil, and he will flee from you.

DEDICATIONS

I'm dedicating this book first and foremost to Jesus Christ, my Lord and Saviour and father. I am a child of God.

I am also dedicating this book to my Mom for her guidance in my young life and teaching me about God. She taught me to live a good life with Christian values instilled deeply within my soul and my heart until I was ready to become a born again Child of God.

And last but not least, I'm dedicating this book to Brenda (BG Jenkins) for being there to answer the hundreds of questions I've had about studying the Bible and being my Sister in Christ.

About The Author

When Did You First Start Writing?

I have always written in journals and diaries to work my way through problems or times that have been upsetting to me.

Writing is a creative outlet and when you write words on paper, they are then released from your thoughts and you are able to create even more.

Why Do You Continue To Write?

Since writing got me through the most trying times of my life and through the grief process after the death of my husband, I found myself coming back to writing day after day.

It feels better to get those thoughts out on paper and in the process; I believe I can help others who may be going through hard times.

Where to Find Monna Ellithorpe Online

Email: mailto:Monna@monnaellithorpe.com or

mailto:monnaellithorpe@gmail.com

Website: http://monnaellithorpe.com

Twitter: http://twitter.com/msellithorpe

Facebook: (Profile Page)

https://www.facebook.com/monna.ellithorpe.1

FB (Fan Page) Monna Ellithorpe – Author & Writer

https://www.facebook.com/monnaellithorpeauthor/

Google+
https://plus.google.com/u/0/+MonnaEllithorpe/posts

LinkedIn:
https://www.linkedin.com/in/monnaellithorpe

Monna Ellithorpe Amazon Author Page:
http://www.ibourl.com/1fs9

THE END

"Saved By His Amazing Grace" is about a series of life-altering events that changed my life in so many ways.

I never dreamed that one day I would be telling people about the Word of God and the amazing way He's touched my life.

Deuteronomy 4:29 (NIV)
"But if from there you seek the LORD your God, you will find Him if you look for Him with all your heart and with all your soul."

Printed in France by Amazon
Brétigny-sur-Orge, FR

29895619R00043